S0-ANO-374

ENDANGERED!

ELEPHANTS

Amanda Harman

Series Consultant: James G. Doherty
General Curator, The Bronx Zoo, New York

BENCHMARK BOOKS

MARSHALL CAVENDISH
NEW YORK

Benchmark Books
Marshall Cavendish Corporation
99 White Plains Road
Tarrytown, New York 10591-9001

Library of Congress Cataloging-in-Publication Data

Harman, Amanda, 1968
    Elephants / Amanda Harman.
        p.   cm. — (Endangered!)
    Includes bibliographical references and index.
    Summary: Provides descriptions of the physical characteristics and
habits of both Asian and African elephants.
    ISBN 0-7614-0221-7 (lib. bdg.)
    1. Elephants—Juvenile literature.   2. Endangered species—
Juvenile literature.   [1. Elephants. 2. Endangered species.]
I. Title.   II. Series.
QL737.P98H368 1996
599.6'1—dc20   95-39909
                                                 CIP
                                                 AC

Printed in Hong Kong

PICTURE CREDITS
*The publishers would like to thank the Frank Lane Picture Agency (FLPA) for
supplying all the photographs used in this book except for the following:* 1, 20,
22, 23, 24, 26 Silvestris (via FLPA); 24 Bruce Coleman.

Series created by Brown Packaging

Front cover: African elephant.
Title page: Asian elephants.
Back cover: African elephants.

Contents

Elephants are the largest land animals. They are twice as heavy as the second largest – the hippopotamus – and more than two million times larger than the smallest land mammal – the pygmy white-toothed shrew. This is an African elephant.

Introduction

Everyone knows what an elephant looks like. With its long trunk and big ears, the elephant is one of the most familiar animals in the world. For many years this big, gray, lumbering creature has entertained us at zoos and circuses. But in the wild, these intelligent, gentle giants are dying out very quickly. Soon they may be completely **extinct**.

Like human beings, elephants are **mammals**. They have hair on their skin and feed their babies with milk. Though they may weigh several tons, elephants are surprisingly light on their feet. They move fairly quietly and leave hardly any footprints behind. This is because their round feet are wide, with soft, fleshy pads on the bottom.

The elephant's most distinctive feature is its trunk, which can be over 7 feet (2.1 m) long. This is the elephant's nose, through which the animal breathes and smells. It can be used for other things, too, such as gathering food. An elephant can also use its trunk as a hose for sucking up water to drink or to shower with. The trunk is so large, it can draw in up to 14.5 gallons (55 liters) of water at one

Using its trunk like a long arm with a hand on the end, an African elephant picks leaves from high up in the trees.

time. It is made completely of muscle and has no bones. An elephant's trunk is so strong, it can lift whole tree trunks into the air. And it is so sensitive, it can easily pick up an egg or a small coin.

Elephants are also well known for their tusks, though not all elephants have them. Those that do are born with them, and they continue to grow throughout the animals' lifetime. Just as people are either right- or left-handed, so elephants use one of their tusks more than the other.

A female Asian elephant with her small tusks just showing below her lip. Tusks are actually long, pointed upper teeth.

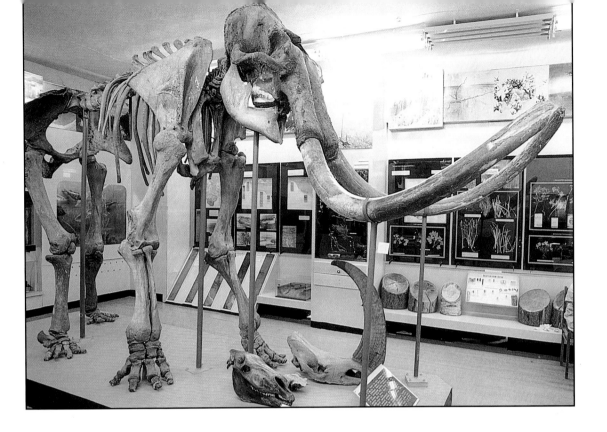

Today there are just two **species** of elephants: the African elephant and the Asian elephant. At one time, there were many more, but the last of these other kinds – the mammoths – died out thousands of years ago. Mammoths vanished largely because they could not **adapt** to natural changes in their environment after the **Ice Age** ended. However, some scientists think that early human hunters may have helped to kill off the mammoths, too.

Hunting is one of the major reasons that modern-day elephants are in danger. The other is that people keep moving into areas where elephants live, leaving them without a home. In this book, we will learn all about elephants and about what can be done to prevent these wonderful creatures from disappearing forever.

A mammoth skeleton in a museum. Some mammoths lived near the Arctic and had coats of long, shaggy hair to help them survive in cold conditions.

Areas where the
African elephant
can be found

African Elephant

The African elephant is found in many parts of Africa
south of the Sahara Desert. It lives on **savannas**, grasslands
where trees are few and widely scattered. In some parts of
its **range**, it also lives in the **rainforest**.

African elephants have very big ears. They have to put
up with the blazing heat of the open savannas, and their
ears act as a cooling system, allowing body heat to escape.
Elephants can also wave their large ears back and forth like
huge fans to waft cooling air over their body.

African elephants can be 13 feet (4 m) tall at the
shoulders. Males usually weigh about 11,000 pounds

*African
elephants have
rounded
heads, and
their trunks
end in two
"lips" that can
be used like
fingers.*

(5000 kg), though the largest ever known was close to 27,000 pounds (12,275 kg). Females are smaller and weigh about 6600 pounds (3000 kg).

Despite being so big, elephants are very peaceful creatures. They are **herbivores**, which means that they eat plants and do not hunt and kill other animals for food. Elephants eat a wide range of plant food. Besides feeding on grasses and leaves from bushes and trees, they eat small twigs and branches, tree bark, flowers, fruit, and seeds.

An African elephant and a band of olive baboons feeding on palm fruits.

African Elephant

Plant material is very tough to eat, and it soon wears down an elephant's teeth. Besides their tusks, elephants have four teeth, one on each side of their upper and lower jaw. Like everything else about them, elephants' teeth are big. They are about 12 inches (30 cm) long – that's about as long as your hand and forearm from the tip of your fingers to your elbow. Each tooth has ridges for grinding down grass and leaves. As a tooth begins to wear out, it moves forward to the front of the elephant's mouth, as if it were on a conveyor belt, and a new one starts growing to

Elephants even use their trunks when feeding on grass. They have short necks and can't reach the ground with their mouths.

take its place. Once the new tooth is ready, the worn-out tooth drops out. Elephants have up to six sets of teeth in a lifetime. Once their last set has worn out, elephants can no longer eat, and they die of starvation.

Because they are so big, African elephants need to eat a huge amount. A large male may eat more than 495 pounds (225 kg) of food a day just to keep alive. He may also drink as much as 40 gallons (150 liters) of water. To satisfy their great appetites, elephants sometimes spend as many as

Elephants can cause great damage to plants and trees. These two are stripping a trunk of its bark. This will kill the tree.

11

20 hours a day searching for and eating food. They move
through the countryside, often snatching at food and eating
it as they walk. Elephants walk at an average speed of
about 15 miles per hour (24 km/h). Sometimes they cover
up to 50 miles (80 km) in a single day.

Although African elephants may wander great distances,
they never move far away from water. Besides needing
water to drink, elephants like to bathe. After their bath, the
elephants suck up dust in their trunks and then spray it over
their bodies. This protects them from insect bites. An
elephant's skin is sensitive, despite being over 1.5 inches
(4 cm) thick in places. In the dry season, when there is not

A young elephant enjoys a bath. Elephants love water and may bathe for hours on end.

enough water around for a bath, elephants suck up a little water in their trunks and give themselves a shower instead. Sometimes they also dig for water in sandy riverbeds.

Female elephants are known as cows, and young elephants are called calves. African cow elephants and their young live in family groups of eight to ten. Each group is led by a female, known as the **matriarch**. The matriarch is usually the oldest female in the group and may be over 60 years old. Since elephants continue to grow throughout their lifetime, this means she is usually the biggest, too.

Besides digging for water, elephants dig up and eat soil. In soil they find the salt and other minerals they need to stay healthy.

Elephants do not see very well, but their hearing is excellent. As they search for food, members of a family group keep in contact with one another by making low "rumbling" noises. Elephants can hear these rumbles up to 6 miles (9.7 km) away. If they sense danger, the elephants let the rest of the group know by suddenly stopping the rumbling noises. Elephants also have a well-developed sense of smell. You can often see African elephants lifting their trunks to sniff the air for danger.

Whenever enemies, such as lions, approach, the elephants immediately surround their babies to protect

Elephants are very social animals and look after one another and their young. Here, a group of adults helps a young elephant to cross a river.

them. Then the adults warn the intruders to leave by making special threatening signals, including whirling their trunks in the air, beating them against the ground, or using them to pick up and throw dust. They also fan their ears out as far as they can to make themselves look bigger and more frightening and make "trumpeting" calls. If the enemies do not turn and go away, the elephants may charge at them. A charging African elephant can run as fast as 20 miles per hour (32 km/h) – an awesome and terrifying sight!

Usually, the only males found in these family groups are young ones. Once they reach about 12 years old, they leave the group and live either alone or in all-male groups. Adult male elephants are called bulls. From time to time, a

A group of male African elephants in their savanna home. All-male groups are usually smaller than family groups.

number of family groups and bull elephants gather together to form a large herd. African elephant herds can contain up to 1000 animals, so they usually form only where there is plenty of food for the elephants to eat.

Besides lions and other large meat-eating animals, which might kill the babies, an African elephant's main enemies are people. This is because people hunt elephants for their tusks. Elephant tusks are made from a hard, creamy-white substance called ivory, which is very valuable. People use it to make ornaments and jewelry. The white keys on pianos often used to be made of this material and are

An elephant comes face to face with an angry rhinoceros. Rhinos are large, fast, and fearless and may charge an elephant that comes too close.

commonly called "ivories" for that reason. Male African elephants have very large tusks. At the age of 60, a bull's tusks may weigh 130 pounds (60 kg) each, although the heaviest of all time weighed almost 260 pounds (118 kg)!

Sadly, people can get the tusks only by killing the elephants first. Over the years, huge numbers of these gentle creatures have died, just for ivory. By 1903, elephants had almost disappeared from southern Africa, and the number of elephants in other areas of Africa was also falling fast. Despite this, people demanded more ivory, and the killing continued. During the 1980s alone, elephant hunters sold thousands of tons of ivory to foreign countries. In that time, African elephant numbers dropped from over

An elephant lies dead, killed by illegal ivory hunters. The killers must have been frightened off by guards before they could take the elephant's tusks.

one million to just over 600,000. In 1989, **conservationists** announced that the African elephant was in great danger of becoming extinct. The same year, governments around the world agreed to make selling ivory against the law.

Elephant numbers have increased in southern Africa since then. But **poachers** still hunt elephants, and in other parts of Africa numbers are still falling. Many of the African countries in which elephants live are poor, and a poacher can earn a lot of money by killing an elephant and selling its tusks. Conservationists have tried to keep elephants in protected areas, such as **reserves** and national parks. However, it is very difficult to provide areas that are

A store of ivory taken from poachers in Tanzania, East Africa. The huge tusk on the right of the picture would have been worth an enormous sum.

big enough to contain enough food for these huge animals. As we have seen, elephants have enormous appetites, and they soon eat all the vegetation in the national park or reserve. Many of them then starve or break out of their protected area. Once outside, the elephants are more difficult to protect from poachers. To make matters worse, poachers also enter the parks and kill the elephants inside. The African elephant is still threatened with extinction.

An elephant herd on the move. African elephants' home areas can cover over 1000 square miles (2600 sq km).

Areas where the
Asian elephant can
be found

Asian Elephant

About 17 million years ago, elephants from the plains of
Africa traveled to Asia, where they made their homes
mainly in forests. Over many thousands of years, the Asian
elephant developed from these original animals. Today,
Asian elephants are smaller than African elephants. Males
are usually about 10 feet (2.9 m) high at the shoulders –
though they can be taller – and may weigh up to 11,000
pounds (5000 kg).

   Besides being smaller than its African cousin, the Asian
elephant is different in shape. Also, an Asian elephant's

*An Asian
elephant
showering or
perhaps just
playing. Light-
colored skin
on the ears
and trunk is
fairly common
in Asian
elephants.*

trunk has only one "lip" or "finger" at the tip whereas the African's has two. Asian elephants usually have smaller tusks than African elephants do. Most Asian bulls have tusks, and some females grow them, too. However, female tusks are often so small they do not show. Asian elephants live mainly in rainforests and are found in India, Sri Lanka, Southeast Asia, and on the Indonesian island of Sumatra.

Asian cow elephants live in family groups of four to eight animals. Two or more of these groups may sometimes form a small herd. Elephants are caring animals. If a member of the group is sick or wounded, the rest comfort it by stroking it with their trunks. If one of the group is injured or dying, the rest refuse to leave it. This may put

An Asian bull elephant. The Asian elephant has a more dome-shaped head than the African elephant and a rounder body with a humped back.

the elephants in danger, especially if there are hunters nearby. It is said that after an elephant dies, the other members of the family group grieve for their lost friend. Some people claim that elephants cry when they are upset.

There are also many stories of elephants going to special "elephant graveyards" to die. It is true that large piles of elephant bones are often found in one place. Scientists have tried to find out why this is so. One idea is that a "graveyard" is a place where a whole group of elephants died at once. The group may have gone there hoping to find water or food in the dry season, found nothing, and then died of thirst or hunger.

Like adult male African elephants, Asian bulls can live alone or in all-male groups. Once or twice a year, bull

A baby Asian elephant nuzzles up to an adult. Elephants are friendly toward other members of their family group. They often touch one another in greeting or out of affection.

elephants experience a strange condition called **musth** (pronounced "must"). When they are in musth, fluid flows from glands between the elephants' eyes and ears. Normally, if two elephants have a disagreement about something, they settle it without fighting. Musth, however, can make bulls very aggressive toward one another. At one time scientists thought that only Asian bull elephants came into musth, but they now know that African bulls do, too.

Bull elephants can also become violent when there are female elephants around that are ready to breed. Two male rivals may fight for the right to **mate** with a particular female. One bull may wrap its trunk around the other's, or the two elephants may lock their tusks together, each trying to make the other lose its balance. Sometimes they charge

A bull Asian elephant raises its trunk as a warning to stay away.

23

*Two young
Asian bulls
tussle with
each other.
This is just
play. It is also
training,
though, for the
day they may
fight in earnest
over a female.*

at high speed and crash their heads together or stab at each other with their long, pointed tusks. These fights can last up to six hours.

Once the fight has been settled, the winner mates with the female. Afterward, the bull goes away. It takes no part in bringing up the calf once it is born. Elephant pregnancies last about two years – more than twice as long as human ones. The calves are usually born in the rainy season, when there is plenty of food available. When the cow is ready to give birth, the rest of the elephants in the group often gather around to protect her from enemies. Another female elephant helps at the birth. Sometimes the helper is the leader of the herd; other times she is a special "midwife" elephant. The mother usually has only one calf – an Asian elephant weighs about 200 pounds (90 kg) at birth! All the other females in the family group welcome the new baby by stroking it gently with their trunks.

For the first year, the young elephant calf is small enough to walk along under its mother's belly when the group is on the move. This is where the calf feels safest. Elephant calves grow very quickly. By the time they are six years old, young Asian elephants weigh about a ton. Like many baby mammals, young elephants spend much of their time playing together. They have lots of fun, throwing pieces of wood around, splashing in water, wallowing in

A baby trots along with its mother. Asian elephants are walking within two hours of being born. They need to be, since there may be a hungry tiger nearby.

mud, and chasing one another. Playing helps them to learn important skills, such as how to use their trunks. It also teaches young males which of them is the strongest.

People have long had a close relationship with the Asian elephant. For at least 3500 years, they have tamed these gentle creatures. They have trained them to perform tricks in zoos and circuses and to transport people and heavy loads. Not all people like elephants, however. Farmers sometimes shoot them because elephants destroy their crops. Other people are simply afraid of elephants because

An elephant at work, loading cut trees onto a truck. Asian elephants are extremely intelligent and can be trained quickly.

they are so large and powerful. Elephants can sometimes be dangerous if they are scared or angry. In India alone, over 200 people have been killed by elephants in a single year.

Sadly, the Asian elephant is even more endangered than the African, but not for the same reasons. Because Asian elephants usually have small tusks, they are in less danger from ivory poachers. Instead, the main threat to the Asian elephant is the loss of its **habitat**. People are cutting down Asian forests at a fast rate. They are collecting timber to sell to other countries or clearing land so people can build villages, plant crops, and graze their farm animals. There may be fewer than 35,000 Asian elephants left in the wild.

However, people are taking steps to help the Asian elephant. In Sri Lanka, for example, when areas of elephant habitat are cut down, people are leaving corridors between

Two Asian elephants take a bath while their masters wait nearby. An elephant and its master have a close relationship. A well-trained elephant always responds to its master's voice, even in a noisy place.

27

one area and another. This allows elephants to continue to move safely from place to place. Without corridors, elephants would be cut off from some of their feeding areas and from others of their own kind. They would not keep breeding and so would eventually die out.

Elsewhere in Asia, people are digging extra waterholes and planting trees in elephant areas. This creates more food and water so that greater numbers of elephants can live there. Meanwhile, in Malaysia, when forests are cut down for rubber or palm plantations, the elephants are captured. Conservationists take them to another part of the forest and then release them back into the wild.

Tourists ride an elephant in India's Kaziranga National Park, which also contains wild elephants. This is one of several places in Asia where wild elephants can live safely.

Both species of elephants are still in danger. As we have seen, in the case of the African elephant, poaching for ivory is the problem; in the case of the Asian elephant, habitat loss is mainly to blame. Conservationists have worked hard to warn the world that elephants are at risk and to find ways to protect them. Many people have listened and are putting these plans into action. Because of this, there is a good chance that elephants will be walking the grasslands and forest trails of the future.

A young Asian elephant feeding at the edge of a waterhole. Elephants need people's help if they are to survive.

Useful Addresses

For more information about elephants and how you can help protect them, contact these organizations:

Conservation International
1015 18th Street NW
Suite 1000
Washington, D.C. 20036

Elephant Research Foundation
106 East Hickory Grove
Bloomfield Hills, MI 48304

U.S. Fish and Wildlife Service
Endangered Species and Habitat
Conservation
400 Arlington Square
18th and C Streets NW
Washington, D.C. 20240

The Wildlife Conservation Society
185th Street and Southern Boulevard
Bronx, New York 10460

Wildlife Preservation Trust International
3400 W Girard Avenue
Philadelphia, PA 19104

World Wildlife Fund
1250 24th Street NW
Washington, D.C. 20037

World Wildlife Fund Canada
90 Eglinton Avenue East
Suite 504
Toronto
Ontario M4P 2Z7

Further Reading

African Elephants: Giants of the Land Dorothy Hinshaw Patent (New York: Holiday House, 1991)

The Elephant Family Olivia Douglas-Hamilton (Saxonville, MA: Picture Book Studio, 1990)

Endangered Wildlife of the World (New York: Marshall Cavendish Corporation, 1993)

Operation Elephant Jill Bailey (Austin, TX: Raintree Steck-Vaughn, 1994)

Wildlife of the World (New York: Marshall Cavendish Corporation, 1994)

The World of Elephants Virginia Harrison (Milwaukee: Gareth Stevens, 1990)

Glossary

Adapt: To change in order to survive in new conditions.

Conservationist (Kon-ser-VAY-shun-ist): A person who protects and preserves the Earth's natural resources, such as animals, plants, and soil.

Extinct (Ex-TINKT): No longer living anywhere in the world.

Habitat: The place where an animal lives. The Asian elephant's habitat is the rainforest.

Herbivore (HER-biv-or): A kind of animal that eats plants rather than animals.

Ice Age: The period in the Earth's history when the climate was very cold, and ice covered much of the planet. The Ice Age ended about 10,000 years ago.

Mammal: A kind of animal that is warm-blooded and has a backbone. Most are covered with fur or have hair. Females have glands that produce milk to feed their young.

Mate: When a male and female get together to produce young.

Matriarch (MAY-tree-ark): The female leader of a family group of elephants.

Musth (Must): A condition experienced by male elephants once or twice a year. Fluid flows from glands between the eyes and ears, and the elephants can become aggressive.

Poacher: A person who hunts animals even though it is against the law.

Rainforest: A forest that has heavy rainfall much of the year.

Range: The area in the world in which a particular kind of animal can be found.

Reserve: Land that has been set aside where plants and animals can live without being harmed.

Savanna: Wide open plains found near the Equator. Grass is the main type of plant, and trees are few and widely scattered.

Species: A kind of animal or plant. For example, the African and Asian elephant are two different species of elephants.

Index